Sweet *or* SPICY?

MORE
QUICK QUIZZES
FOR BFFS

To Britt, and only Britt—you're the best!

—L.M.

ISBN-13: 978-0-545-15603-5

ISBN-10: 0-545-15603-3

12 11 10 9 8 7 6 5 4 3   10 11 12 13 14/0

Printed in the U.S.A.   40

First printing, November 2009

Illustrations and book design by Janet Kusmierski

Sweet or Spicy?

BY LIZZIE MACK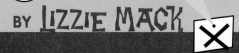

SCHOLASTIC INC.

New York   Toronto   London   Auckland
Sydney   Mexico City   New Delhi   Hong Kong

What superpower would you love to have?

What is the most important quality in a friend?

Would you rather have a puppy or a kitten?

Are you a risk-taker or do you like to play it safe?

These questions and more are here for you to answer with your best buds.

Take the quizzes (some involve difficult—LOL—choices), then share and compare!

ENJOY!

PERSONALITY QUIRKS
Mirror, mirror, looking inside . . .

1. Do you have boys as friends? ◯ Yes or ◯ Eww, no way!

2. Do you ◯ Like it quiet or ◯ Need something going on?

3. Would you ◯ Ask a boy to dance or ◯ Wait to be asked?

4. ◯ Shy or ◯ Talk to everybody?

5. ◯ Day or ◯ Night?

6. ◯ Truth or ◯ Dare?

7. What "truth" question would you ask?

   _____

8. What kind of a dare would you give?

   _____

9. Are you ◯ A daydreamer or ◯ All business?

10. Love at first sight? ◯ Absolutely (sigh...) or

    ◯ No! Life's not a fairy tale.

11. ◯ Do you love the drama or ◯ Would you rather

    everybody just got along?

12. What one word would your parents use to describe you?

    _____

13. What one word would your friends use to describe you?

    _____

14. What one word would you use to describe yourself?

    _____

15. Do you believe in miracles? ◯ Yes ◯ No or ◯ Depends

16. Do you ◯ Break a rule now and then or ◯ Get too nervous to even cut in line?

17. Do you prefer ◯ Spicy salsa and chips or ◯ Cupcakes with buttercream frosting?

18. Would you rather have ◯ Sour apple candy or ◯ A Granny Smith apple?

19. ◯ Fly or ◯ Be able to breathe underwater?

20. ◯ Super-strong or ◯ Super-smart?

21. ◯ X-ray vision or ◯ Supersonic hearing?

22. ◯ Read minds or ◯ See the future?

23. Would you rather have ◯ Hands that can heal or ◯ Hands that turn things to gold?

24. Do you ◯ Smile all the time or ◯ Always act serious and mature?

25. Would you rather ◯ Run around outside ◯ Watch television or ◯ Play on the computer?

26. Would you rather be a ◯ Lion or ◯ Tiger?

27. ◯ Mustang convertible or ◯ VW Bug?

28. ◯ Dog or ◯ Cat?

29. ◯ Movie star or ◯ Nobel Prize winner?

30. ◯ Daisy or ◯ Oak tree?

PERSONALITY QUIRKS
Mirror, mirror, looking inside . . .

1. Do you have boys as friends? ◯ Yes or ◯ Eww, no way!

2. Do you ◯ Like it quiet or ◯ Need something going on?

3. Would you ◯ Ask a boy to dance or ◯ Wait to be asked?

4. ◯ Shy or ◯ Talk to everybody?

5. ◯ Day or ◯ Night?

6. ◯ Truth or ◯ Dare?

7. What "truth" question would you ask?

   _____

8. What kind of a dare would you give?

   _____

9. Are you ◯ A daydreamer or ◯ All business?

10. Love at first sight? ◯ Absolutely (sigh...) or

    ◯ No! Life's not a fairy tale.

11. ◯ Do you love the drama or ◯ Would you rather

    everybody just got along?

12. What one word would your parents use to describe you?

    _____

13. What one word would your friends use to describe you?

    _____

14. What one word would you use to describe yourself?

    _____

15. Do you believe in miracles? ◯ Yes ◯ No or ◯ Depends

16. Do you ◯ Break a rule now and then or ◯ Get too nervous to even cut in line?

17. Do you prefer ◯ Spicy salsa and chips or ◯ Cupcakes with buttercream frosting?

18. Would you rather have ◯ Sour apple candy or ◯ A Granny Smith apple?

19. ◯ Fly or ◯ Be able to breathe underwater?

20. ◯ Super-strong or ◯ Super-smart?

21. ◯ X-ray vision or ◯ Supersonic hearing?

22. ◯ Read minds or ◯ See the future?

23. Would you rather have ◯ Hands that can heal or ◯ Hands that turn things to gold?

24. Do you ◯ Smile all the time or ◯ Always act serious and mature?

25. Would you rather ◯ Run around outside ◯ Watch television or ◯ Play on the computer?

26. Would you rather be a ◯ Lion or ◯ Tiger?

27. ◯ Mustang convertible or ◯ VW Bug?

28. ◯ Dog or ◯ Cat?

29. ◯ Movie star or ◯ Nobel Prize winner?

30. ◯ Daisy or ◯ Oak tree?

PERSONALITY QUIRKS

Mirror, mirror, looking inside . . .

1. Do you have boys as friends? ⚪ Yes or ⚪ Eww, no way!

2. Do you ⚪ Like it quiet or ⚪ Need something going on?

3. Would you ⚪ Ask a boy to dance or ⚪ Wait to be asked?

4. ⚪ Shy or ⚪ Talk to everybody?

5. ⚪ Day or ⚪ Night?

6. ⚪ Truth or ⚪ Dare?

7. What "truth" question would you ask?

_____

8. What kind of a dare would you give?

_____

9. Are you ⚪ A daydreamer or ⚪ All business?

10. Love at first sight? ⚪ Absolutely (sigh...) or

    ⚪ No! Life's not a fairy tale.

11. ⚪ Do you love the drama or ⚪ Would you rather

    everybody just got along?

12. What one word would your parents use to describe you?

_____

13. What one word would your friends use to describe you?

_____

14. What one word would you use to describe yourself?

_____

15. Do you believe in miracles? ⚪ Yes ⚪ No or ⚪ Depends

16. Do you ◯ Break a rule now and then or ◯ Get too nervous to even cut in line?

17. Do you prefer ◯ Spicy salsa and chips or ◯ Cupcakes with buttercream frosting?

18. Would you rather have ◯ Sour apple candy or ◯ A Granny Smith apple?

19. ◯ Fly or ◯ Be able to breathe underwater?

20. ◯ Super-strong or ◯ Super-smart?

21. ◯ X-ray vision or ◯ Supersonic hearing?

22. ◯ Read minds or ◯ See the future?

23. Would you rather have ◯ Hands that can heal or ◯ Hands that turn things to gold?

24. Do you ◯ Smile all the time or ◯ Always act serious and mature?

25. Would you rather ◯ Run around outside ◯ Watch television or ◯ Play on the computer?

26. Would you rather be a ◯ Lion or ◯ Tiger?

27. ◯ Mustang convertible or ◯ VW Bug?

28. ◯ Dog or ◯ Cat?

29. ◯ Movie star or ◯ Nobel Prize winner?

30. ◯ Daisy or ◯ Oak tree?

PERSONALITY QUIRKS
Mirror, mirror, looking inside . . .

1. Do you have boys as friends? ◯ Yes or ◯ Eww, no way!

2. Do you ◯ Like it quiet or ◯ Need something going on?

3. Would you ◯ Ask a boy to dance or ◯ Wait to be asked?

4. ◯ Shy or ◯ Talk to everybody?

5. ◯ Day or ◯ Night?

6. ◯ Truth or ◯ Dare?

7. What "truth" question would you ask?

   _____

8. What kind of a dare would you give?

   _____

9. Are you ◯ A daydreamer or ◯ All business?

10. Love at first sight? ◯ Absolutely (sigh...) or

    ◯ No! Life's not a fairy tale.

11. ◯ Do you love the drama or ◯ Would you rather

    everybody just got along?

12. What one word would your parents use to describe you?

    _____

13. What one word would your friends use to describe you?

    _____

14. What one word would you use to describe yourself?

    _____

15. Do you believe in miracles? ◯ Yes ◯ No or ◯ Depends

16. Do you ◯ Break a rule now and then or ◯ Get too nervous to even cut in line?

17. Do you prefer ◯ Spicy salsa and chips or ◯ Cupcakes with buttercream frosting?

18. Would you rather have ◯ Sour apple candy or ◯ A Granny Smith apple?

19. ◯ Fly or ◯ Be able to breathe underwater?

20. ◯ Super-strong or ◯ Super-smart?

21. ◯ X-ray vision or ◯ Supersonic hearing?

22. ◯ Read minds or ◯ See the future?

23. Would you rather have ◯ Hands that can heal or ◯ Hands that turn things to gold?

24. Do you ◯ Smile all the time or ◯ Always act serious and mature?

25. Would you rather ◯ Run around outside ◯ Watch television or ◯ Play on the computer?

26. Would you rather be a ◯ Lion or ◯ Tiger?

27. ◯ Mustang convertible or ◯ VW Bug?

28. ◯ Dog or ◯ Cat?

29. ◯ Movie star or ◯ Nobel Prize winner?

30. ◯ Daisy or ◯ Oak tree?

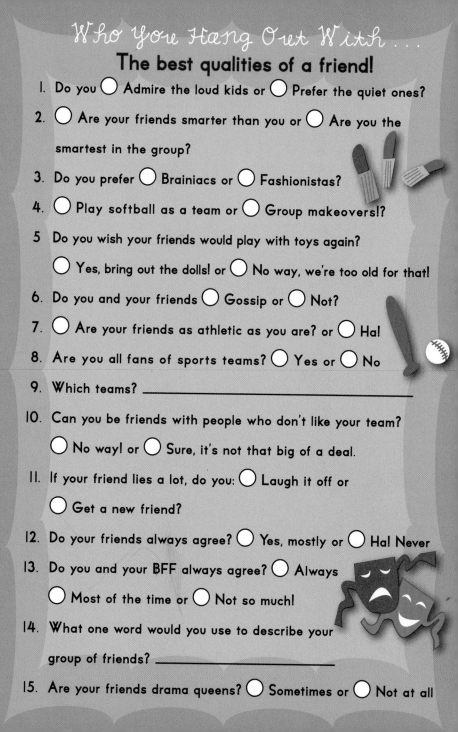

Who You Hang Out With...
The best qualities of a friend!

1. Do you ◯ Admire the loud kids or ◯ Prefer the quiet ones?

2. ◯ Are your friends smarter than you or ◯ Are you the smartest in the group?

3. Do you prefer ◯ Brainiacs or ◯ Fashionistas?

4. ◯ Play softball as a team or ◯ Group makeovers!?

5. Do you wish your friends would play with toys again?

   ◯ Yes, bring out the dolls! or ◯ No way, we're too old for that!

6. Do you and your friends ◯ Gossip or ◯ Not?

7. ◯ Are your friends as athletic as you are? or ◯ Ha!

8. Are you all fans of sports teams? ◯ Yes or ◯ No

9. Which teams? _____

10. Can you be friends with people who don't like your team?

    ◯ No way! or ◯ Sure, it's not that big of a deal.

11. If your friend lies a lot, do you: ◯ Laugh it off or
    ◯ Get a new friend?

12. Do your friends always agree? ◯ Yes, mostly or ◯ Ha! Never

13. Do you and your BFF always agree? ◯ Always
    ◯ Most of the time or ◯ Not so much!

14. What one word would you use to describe your group of friends? _____

15. Are your friends drama queens? ◯ Sometimes or ◯ Not at all

16. Would they rather buy ⃝ A book or ⃝ Hair accessories?

17. Would they rather ⃝ Listen to music or ⃝ Sing together?

18. If you are crushing on somebody, do your friends ⃝ Tease you or ⃝ Support you?

19. One word to describe your BFF: _____

20. One thing in your BFF's wardrobe you want: _____

21. One thing you admire about your BFF: _____

22. If you could trade one feature with your best friend, would it be: ⃝ Hair ⃝ Eye color or ⃝ Height?

23. Do you ⃝ Compete with friends or ⃝ Just chill out?

24. Have you and your BFF ever competed against each other? ⃝ Yes or ⃝ No

25. Were you mean? ⃝ Yes, a little or ⃝ No, we handled it.

26. What would happen if you and your BFF liked the same boy?

_____

27. Would your friends go bungee jumping with you if you asked them? ⃝ Ha! ⃝ Maybe or ⃝ Sure!

28. Would your friends try out for the school play if you asked them? ⃝ Never! ⃝ Maybe or ⃝ Absolutely!

29. Would your friends wear their pajamas to school with you? ⃝ Um . . . ⃝ No way! or ⃝ Of course!

30. Who is your most daring friend?_____

Who You Hang Out With...
The best qualities of a friend!

1. Do you ⭕ Admire the loud kids or ⭕ Prefer the quiet ones?

2. ⭕ Are your friends smarter than you or ⭕ Are you the smartest in the group?

3. Do you prefer ⭕ Brainiacs or ⭕ Fashionistas?

4. ⭕ Play softball as a team or ⭕ Group makeovers!?

5. Do you wish your friends would play with toys again?

   ⭕ Yes, bring out the dolls! or ⭕ No way, we're too old for that!

6. Do you and your friends ⭕ Gossip or ⭕ Not?

7. ⭕ Are your friends as athletic as you are? or ⭕ Ha!

8. Are you all fans of sports teams? ⭕ Yes or ⭕ No

9. Which teams? _____

10. Can you be friends with people who don't like your team?

    ⭕ No way! or ⭕ Sure, it's not that big of a deal.

11. If your friend lies a lot, do you: ⭕ Laugh it off or

    ⭕ Get a new friend?

12. Do your friends always agree? ⭕ Yes, mostly or ⭕ Ha! Never

13. Do you and your BFF always agree? ⭕ Always

    ⭕ Most of the time or ⭕ Not so much!

14. What one word would you use to describe your group of friends? _____

15. Are your friends drama queens? ⭕ Sometimes or ⭕ Not at all

16. Would they rather buy ⭕ A book or ⭕ Hair accessories?

17. Would they rather ⭕ Listen to music or ⭕ Sing together?

18. If you are crushing on somebody, do your friends
    ⭕ Tease you or ⭕ Support you?

19. One word to describe your BFF: _____

20. One thing in your BFF's wardrobe you want: _____

21. One thing you admire about your BFF: _____

22. If you could trade one feature with your best friend,
    would it be: ⭕ Hair ⭕ Eye color or ⭕ Height?

23. Do you ⭕ Compete with friends or ⭕ Just chill out?

24. Have you and your BFF ever competed against
    each other? ⭕ Yes or ⭕ No

25. Were you mean? ⭕ Yes, a little or ⭕ No, we handled it.

26. What would happen if you and your BFF liked the same boy?
    _____

27. Would your friends go bungee jumping with you if you
    asked them? ⭕ Ha! ⭕ Maybe or ⭕ Sure!

28. Would your friends try out for the school play if you
    asked them? ⭕ Never! ⭕ Maybe or ⭕ Absolutely!

29. Would your friends wear their pajamas to school with
    you? ⭕ Um . . . ⭕ No way! or ⭕ Of course!

30. Who is your most daring friend? _____

The best qualities of a friend!

1. Do you ◯ Admire the loud kids or ◯ Prefer the quiet ones?

2. ◯ Are your friends smarter than you or ◯ Are you the smartest in the group?

3. Do you prefer ◯ Brainiacs or ◯ Fashionistas?

4. ◯ Play softball as a team or ◯ Group makeovers!?

5. Do you wish your friends would play with toys again?

   ◯ Yes, bring out the dolls! or ◯ No way, we're too old for that!

6. Do you and your friends ◯ Gossip or ◯ Not?

7. ◯ Are your friends as athletic as you are? or ◯ Ha!

8. Are you all fans of sports teams? ◯ Yes or ◯ No

9. Which teams? _____

10. Can you be friends with people who don't like your team?

    ◯ No way! or ◯ Sure, it's not that big of a deal.

11. If your friend lies a lot, do you: ◯ Laugh it off or

    ◯ Get a new friend?

12. Do your friends always agree? ◯ Yes, mostly or ◯ Ha! Never

13. Do you and your BFF always agree? ◯ Always

    ◯ Most of the time or ◯ Not so much!

14. What one word would you use to describe your

    group of friends? _____

15. Are your friends drama queens? ◯ Sometimes or ◯ Not at all

16. Would they rather buy ⭕ A book or ⭕ Hair accessories?

17. Would they rather ⭕ Listen to music or ⭕ Sing together?

18. If you are crushing on somebody, do your friends ⭕ Tease you or ⭕ Support you?

19. One word to describe your BFF: _____

20. One thing in your BFF's wardrobe you want: _____

21. One thing you admire about your BFF: _____

22. If you could trade one feature with your best friend, would it be: ⭕ Hair ⭕ Eye color or ⭕ Height?

23. Do you ⭕ Compete with friends or ⭕ Just chill out?

24. Have you and your BFF ever competed against each other? ⭕ Yes or ⭕ No

25. Were you mean? ⭕ Yes, a little or ⭕ No, we handled it.

26. What would happen if you and your BFF liked the same boy? _____

27. Would your friends go bungee jumping with you if you asked them? ⭕ Ha! ⭕ Maybe or ⭕ Sure!

28. Would your friends try out for the school play if you asked them? ⭕ Never! ⭕ Maybe or ⭕ Absolutely!

29. Would your friends wear their pajamas to school with you? ⭕ Um . . . ⭕ No way! or ⭕ Of course!

30. Who is your most daring friend? _____

Who You Hang Out With . . .
The best qualities of a friend!

1. Do you ◯ Admire the loud kids or ◯ Prefer the quiet ones?

2. ◯ Are your friends smarter than you or ◯ Are you the smartest in the group?

3. Do you prefer ◯ Brainiacs or ◯ Fashionistas?

4. ◯ Play softball as a team or ◯ Group makeovers!?

5. Do you wish your friends would play with toys again?

   ◯ Yes, bring out the dolls! or ◯ No way, we're too old for that!

6. Do you and your friends ◯ Gossip or ◯ Not?

7. ◯ Are your friends as athletic as you are? or ◯ Ha!

8. Are you all fans of sports teams? ◯ Yes or ◯ No

9. Which teams? _____

10. Can you be friends with people who don't like your team?

    ◯ No way! or ◯ Sure, it's not that big of a deal.

11. If your friend lies a lot, do you: ◯ Laugh it off or

    ◯ Get a new friend?

12. Do your friends always agree? ◯ Yes, mostly or ◯ Ha! Never

13. Do you and your BFF always agree? ◯ Always

    ◯ Most of the time or ◯ Not so much!

14. What one word would you use to describe your

    group of friends? _____

15. Are your friends drama queens? ◯ Sometimes or ◯ Not at all

16. Would they rather buy ◯ A book or ◯ Hair accessories?

17. Would they rather ◯ Listen to music or ◯ Sing together?

18. If you are crushing on somebody, do your friends
    ◯ Tease you or ◯ Support you?

19. One word to describe your BFF: _____

20. One thing in your BFF's wardrobe you want: _____

21. One thing you admire about your BFF: _____

22. If you could trade one feature with your best friend,
    would it be: ◯ Hair ◯ Eye color or ◯ Height?

23. Do you ◯ Compete with friends or ◯ Just chill out?

24. Have you and your BFF ever competed against
    each other? ◯ Yes or ◯ No

25. Were you mean? ◯ Yes, a little or ◯ No, we handled it.

26. What would happen if you and your BFF liked the same boy?
    _____

27. Would your friends go bungee jumping with you if you
    asked them? ◯ Ha! ◯ Maybe or ◯ Sure!

28. Would your friends try out for the school play if you
    asked them? ◯ Never! ◯ Maybe or ◯ Absolutely!

29. Would your friends wear their pajamas to school with
    you? ◯ Um . . . ◯ No way! or ◯ Of course!

30. Who is your most daring friend? _____

GIRL'S BEST FRIEND

Meow, woof-woof, neigh!

1. Do you have ⦿ Lots of pets ○ Just one or ○ None?

2. Do you have a ⦿ Cat ⦿ Dog ○ Hamster or ⦿ Other?

3. If something unusual, what is it? ___fish tur___

4. Pet name(s): ___Kayley stosh___

5. Did ⦿ You or ○ Your parents or ○ Your siblings name your current pets?

6. What would you name a new pet? ___cocoa___

7. What's your pet's best trick? ___catch___

8. Would you rather have a ○ Kitten or ⦿ Puppy?

9. Would you rather have a ○ Purebred dog or ⦿ Mutt?

10. ○ Labrador or ⦿ Dachshund?

11. ○ Collie or ⦿ Chihuahua?

12. ○ Lazy cat or ⦿ Energetic, playful cat?

13. Would you rather have a ⦿ Horse or ○ Bunny?

14. ○ Guinea pig or ⦿ Hamster?

15. ⦿ Snake or ○ Chameleon?

16. ⊘ Lizard or ◯ Turtle?

17. ◯ Fish or ⊘ Parrot?

18. If you could, would you rather have a ⊘ Koala or ◯ Kangaroo?

19. ⊘ Penguin or ◯ Polar bear?

20. ⊘ Dolphin or ◯ Deer?

21. ◯ Komodo dragon or ⊘ Killer whale?

22. ◯ Raven or ⊘ Reindeer?

23. ◯ Unicorn or ⊘ Pegasus?

24. Do you like horses? ⊘ Absolutely! or ◯ No, I don't understand the attraction!

25. Do you like to ride horses? ⊘ Yes! ◯ No way! or ◯ Only in my dreams!

26. Do you want a horse? ⊘ Absolutely! ◯ Yes, but I'm not allowed to have one or ◯ No!

27. Would you rather ⊘ Walk a dog (remember the pooper scooper!) or ◯ Clean out a cat's litter box?

28. ⊘ Clean out a fish tank or ◯ Feed mice to a snake?

29. ◯ Train a dog to sit or ⊘ Teach a parrot to talk?

30. ◯ Tame a lion or ⊘ Ride an ostrich?

GIRL'S BEST FRIEND

Meow, woof-woof, neigh!

1. Do you have ◯ Lots of pets ◯ Just one or ◯ None?

2. Do you have a ◯ Cat ◯ Dog ◯ Hamster or ◯ Other?

3. If something unusual, what is it? _____

4. Pet name(s): _____

5. Did ◯ You or ◯ Your parents or ◯ Your siblings name your current pets?

6. What would you name a new pet? _____

7. What's your pet's best trick? _____

8. Would you rather have a ◯ Kitten or ◯ Puppy?

9. Would you rather have a ◯ Purebred dog or ◯ Mutt?

10. ◯ Labrador or ◯ Dachshund?

11. ◯ Collie or ◯ Chihuahua?

12. ◯ Lazy cat or ◯ Energetic, playful cat?

13. Would you rather have a ◯ Horse or ◯ Bunny?

14. ◯ Guinea pig or ◯ Hamster?

15. ◯ Snake or ◯ Chameleon?

16. ◯ Lizard or ◯ Turtle?

17. ◯ Fish or ◯ Parrot?

18. If you could, would you rather have a ◯ Koala or ◯ Kangaroo?

19. ◯ Penguin or ◯ Polar bear?

20. ◯ Dolphin or ◯ Deer?

21. ◯ Komodo dragon or ◯ Killer whale?

22. ◯ Raven or ◯ Reindeer?

23. ◯ Unicorn or ◯ Pegasus?

24. Do you like horses? ◯ Absolutely! or ◯ No, I don't understand the attraction!

25. Do you like to ride horses? ◯ Yes! ◯ No way! or ◯ Only in my dreams!

26. Do you want a horse? ◯ Absolutely! ◯ Yes, but I'm not allowed to have one or ◯ No!

27. Would you rather ◯ Walk a dog (remember the pooper scooper!) or ◯ Clean out a cat's litter box?

28. ◯ Clean out a fish tank or ◯ Feed mice to a snake?

29. ◯ Train a dog to sit or ◯ Teach a parrot to talk?

30. ◯ Tame a lion or ◯ Ride an ostrich?

GIRL'S BEST FRIEND

Meow, woof-woof, neigh!

1. Do you have ⭘ Lots of pets ⭘ Just one or ⭘ None?

2. Do you have a ⭘ Cat ⭘ Dog ⭘ Hamster or ⭘ Other?

3. If something unusual, what is it? _____

4. Pet name(s): _____

5. Did ⭘ You or ⭘ Your parents or ⭘ Your siblings name your current pets?

6. What would you name a new pet? _____

7. What's your pet's best trick? _____

8. Would you rather have a ⭘ Kitten or ⭘ Puppy?

9. Would you rather have a ⭘ Purebred dog or ⭘ Mutt?

10. ⭘ Labrador or ⭘ Dachshund?

11. ⭘ Collie or ⭘ Chihuahua?

12. ⭘ Lazy cat or ⭘ Energetic, playful cat?

13. Would you rather have a ⭘ Horse or ⭘ Bunny?

14. ⭘ Guinea pig or ⭘ Hamster?

15. ⭘ Snake or ⭘ Chameleon?

16. ○ Lizard or ○ Turtle?

17. ○ Fish or ○ Parrot?

18. If you could, would you rather have a ○ Koala or ○ Kangaroo?

19. ○ Penguin or ○ Polar bear?

20. ○ Dolphin or ○ Deer?

21. ○ Komodo dragon or ○ Killer whale?

22. ○ Raven or ○ Reindeer?

23. ○ Unicorn or ○ Pegasus?

24. Do you like horses? ○ Absolutely! or ○ No, I don't understand the attraction!

25. Do you like to ride horses? ○ Yes! ○ No way! or ○ Only in my dreams!

26. Do you want a horse? ○ Absolutely! ○ Yes, but I'm not allowed to have one or ○ No!

27. Would you rather ○ Walk a dog (remember the pooper scooper!) or ○ Clean out a cat's litter box?

28. ○ Clean out a fish tank or ○ Feed mice to a snake?

29. ○ Train a dog to sit or ○ Teach a parrot to talk?

30. ○ Tame a lion or ○ Ride an ostrich?

School Daze

Is lunch your favorite subject?

1. Do you like school? ○ Yes, I like to learn!

   ○ No, it's boring or ○ Sure! I get to see my friends!

2. ○ Math or ○ English?

3. Spend the day ○ Reading or ○ Doing a spelling bee?

4. Would you rather spend ○ Two hours in social studies

   or ○ Two hours in science?

5. ○ Do your vocab homework or ○ Wash the dishes?

6. ○ Fractions or ○ Finally clean under your bed?

7. ○ Like your teacher or ○ Not so much!?

8. Is your teacher ○ Fun or ○ Straight by-the-book?

9. Who would you rather have as your teacher?

   _____

10. Would you rather learn ○ French or ○ Spanish?

11. Would you rather ○ Go back to kindergarten or

    ○ Skip ahead to high school?

12. ○ Go to school all year with short vacations between

    quarters or ○ Have a two-and-a-half-month summer vacation?

13. What do you miss about preschool? ○ Naps or ○ Snacks

14. Where do you sit in the cafeteria? ○ Popular table

    ○ Athletes' table ○ With the smart kids or ○ With your friends

15. Do you ○ Bring your lunch or ○ Buy lunch?

1/4

1/2

1/16

school

escuela

ecole

4 X 8 = 32

16. Fave cafeteria food? _____

17. Most disgusting cafeteria food? _____

18. Favorite time period in history?_____

19. Fave person in history? _____

20. If you had dinner with #19, what would you talk about?

_____

21. What is your favorite book? _____

22. Would you rather do ◯ Multiplication and division or

◯ Word problems?

23. Do you know your multiplication tables up to twelve?

◯ Yes or ◯ Are you kidding?

24. What word do you always spell wrong? (We won't

grade you!) _____

25. Which do you like better, ◯ Art or ◯ Music?

26. ◯ Hide in the back of the classroom or ◯ Sit in the

front row?

27. Do you have a locker?_____If yes,

◯ Do you decorate it or ◯ Why bother?

28. Picture day? ◯ Arghllll or ◯ I always look great!

29. Do you ◯ Study for tests or ◯ Just wing it?

30. ◯ Teacher's pet or ◯ Teachers pick on you?

10x2=20

2x16=32

6x4=24

art

music

12
6√72

School Daze
Is lunch your favorite subject?

1. Do you like school? ○ Yes, I like to learn!

   ○ No, it's boring or ○ Sure! I get to see my friends!

2. ○ Math or ○ English?

3. Spend the day ○ Reading or ○ Doing a spelling bee?

4. Would you rather spend ○ Two hours in social studies

   or ○ Two hours in science?

5. ○ Do your vocab homework or ○ Wash the dishes?

6. ○ Fractions or ○ Finally clean under your bed?

7. ○ Like your teacher or ○ Not so much!?

8. Is your teacher ○ Fun or ○ Straight by-the-book?

9. Who would you rather have as your teacher?

   _____

10. Would you rather learn ○ French or ○ Spanish?

11. Would you rather ○ Go back to kindergarten or

    ○ Skip ahead to high school?

12. ○ Go to school all year with short vacations between

    quarters or ○ Have a two-and-a-half-month summer vacation?

13. What do you miss about preschool? ○ Naps or ○ Snacks

14. Where do you sit in the cafeteria? ○ Popular table

    ○ Athletes' table ○ With the smart kids or ○ With your friends

15. Do you ○ Bring your lunch or ○ Buy lunch?

1/4 *1/2* *1/16*

school
escuela
école

4 X 8 = 32

16. Fave cafeteria food? _____

17. Most disgusting cafeteria food? _____

18. Favorite time period in history? _____ 2x16=32

19. Fave person in history? _____ 6x4=24

10x2=20

20. If you had dinner with #19, what would you talk about?

_____

21. What is your favorite book? _____

22. Would you rather do ⭘ Multiplication and division or ⭘ Word problems?

23. Do you know your multiplication tables up to twelve? ⭘ Yes or ⭘ Are you kidding?

art

music

24. What word do you always spell wrong? (We won't grade you!) _____

25. Which do you like better, ⭘ Art or ⭘ Music?

26. ⭘ Hide in the back of the classroom or ⭘ Sit in the front row?

27. Do you have a locker? _____ If yes, ⭘ Do you decorate it or ⭘ Why bother?

28. Picture day? ⭘ Arghllll or ⭘ I always look great!

29. Do you ⭘ Study for tests or ⭘ Just wing it?

30. ⭘ Teacher's pet or ⭘ Teachers pick on you?

12
6√72

School Daze

Is lunch your favorite subject?

1. Do you like school? ◯ Yes, I like to learn!

   ◯ No, it's boring or ◯ Sure! I get to see my friends!

2. ◯ Math or ◯ English?

3. Spend the day ◯ Reading or ◯ Doing a spelling bee?

4. Would you rather spend ◯ Two hours in social studies

   or ◯ Two hours in science?

5. ◯ Do your vocab homework or ◯ Wash the dishes?

6. ◯ Fractions or ◯ Finally clean under your bed?

7. ◯ Like your teacher or ◯ Not so much!?

8. Is your teacher ◯ Fun or ◯ Straight by-the-book?

9. Who would you rather have as your teacher?

   _____

10. Would you rather learn ◯ French or ◯ Spanish?

11. Would you rather ◯ Go back to kindergarten or

    ◯ Skip ahead to high school?

12. ◯ Go to school all year with short vacations between

    quarters or ◯ Have a two-and-a-half-month summer vacation?

13. What do you miss about preschool? ◯ Naps or ◯ Snacks

14. Where do you sit in the cafeteria? ◯ Popular table

    ◯ Athletes' table ◯ With the smart kids or ◯ With your friends

15. Do you ◯ Bring your lunch or ◯ Buy lunch?

1/4

1/2

1/16

school

escuela

ecole

4 X 8 = 32

16. Fave cafeteria food? _____

17. Most disgusting cafeteria food? _____

18. Favorite time period in history?_____

19. Fave person in history? _____

20. If you had dinner with #19, what would you talk about?

    _____

21. What is your favorite book? _____

22. Would you rather do ◯ Multiplication and division or

    ◯ Word problems?

23. Do you know your multiplication tables up to twelve?

    ◯ Yes or ◯ Are you kidding?

24. What word do you always spell wrong? (We won't

    grade you!) _____

25. Which do you like better, ◯ Art or ◯ Music?

26. ◯ Hide in the back of the classroom or ◯ Sit in the

    front row?

27. Do you have a locker?_____If yes,

    ◯ Do you decorate it or ◯ Why bother?

28. Picture day? ◯ Argh!!!! or ◯ I always look great!

29. Do you ◯ Study for tests or ◯ Just wing it?

30. ◯ Teacher's pet or ◯ Teachers pick on you?

10x2=20

2x16=32

6x4=24

art

music

12

6√72

School Daze

Is lunch your favorite subject?

1. Do you like school? ○ Yes, I like to learn!

   ○ No, it's boring or ○ Sure! I get to see my friends!

2. ○ Math or ○ English?

3. Spend the day ○ Reading or ○ Doing a spelling bee?

4. Would you rather spend ○ Two hours in social studies

   or ○ Two hours in science?

5. ○ Do your vocab homework or ○ Wash the dishes?

6. ○ Fractions or ○ Finally clean under your bed?

7. ○ Like your teacher or ○ Not so much!?

8. Is your teacher ○ Fun or ○ Straight by-the-book?

9. Who would you rather have as your teacher?

   _____

10. Would you rather learn ○ French or ○ Spanish?

11. Would you rather ○ Go back to kindergarten or

    ○ Skip ahead to high school?

12. ○ Go to school all year with short vacations between

    quarters or ○ Have a two-and-a-half-month summer vacation?

13. What do you miss about preschool? ○ Naps or ○ Snacks

14. Where do you sit in the cafeteria? ○ Popular table

    ○ Athletes' table ○ With the smart kids or ○ With your friends

15. Do you ○ Bring your lunch or ○ Buy lunch?

1/4

1/2

1/16

school

escuela

ecole

4 X 8 = 32

16. Fave cafeteria food? _____

17. Most disgusting cafeteria food? _____

18. Favorite time period in history?_____

19. Fave person in history? _____ 6x4=24

20. If you had dinner with #19, what would you talk about?

_____

21. What is your favorite book? _____

22. Would you rather do ◯ Multiplication and division or

◯ Word problems? *art*

23. Do you know your multiplication tables up to twelve?

◯ Yes or ◯ Are you kidding? *music*

24. What word do you always spell wrong? (We won't

grade you!) _____

25. Which do you like better, ◯ Art or ◯ Music?

26. ◯ Hide in the back of the classroom or ◯ Sit in the

front row?

27. Do you have a locker?_____If yes,

◯ Do you decorate it or ◯ Why bother?

28. Picture day? ◯ Arghllll or ◯ I always look great!

29. Do you ◯ Study for tests or ◯ Just wing it?

30. ◯ Teacher's pet or ◯ Teachers pick on you?

10x2=20

2x16=32

12
6√72

TAKING CHANCES
Living life on the edge . . .

1. ○ Skydiving or ○ Cliff diving?

2. ○ Parasailing or ○ Hang gliding?

3. ○ Rock climbing or ○ Extreme Rollerblading?

4. Would you rather ○ Be a tiger tamer or ○ Swim with sharks?

5. ○ Ride a bucking horse in a rodeo or ○ Run with the bulls?

6. ○ Go scuba diving or ○ Snorkeling?

7. ○ Walk a tightrope 50 feet in the air or ○ Hang by your legs from a trapeze?

8. Be a crew member ○ On a space shuttle or ○ On a submarine going to the bottom of the ocean?

9. ○ Drive in a NASCAR race or ○ Do some stunt-flying?

10. ○ Ski jump or ○ Surf an aerial on a big wave?

11. ○ Motorcycle or ○ Mountain bike?

12. ○ Bobsled or ○ Luge?

13. ○ Figure skating or ○ Speed skating?

14. ○ Roller coaster or ○ Ferris wheel?

15. ○ Log flume or ○ Lazy river ride?

16. ⭘ Climb giant redwood trees or ⭘ Hike in the Grand Canyon?

17. Fly in a ⭘ Blimp or ⭘ Hot air balloon?

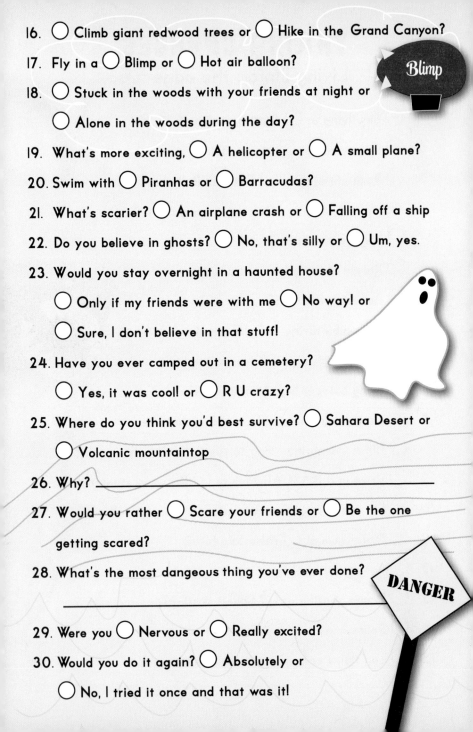

Blimp

18. ⭘ Stuck in the woods with your friends at night or

⭘ Alone in the woods during the day?

19. What's more exciting, ⭘ A helicopter or ⭘ A small plane?

20. Swim with ⭘ Piranhas or ⭘ Barracudas?

21. What's scarier? ⭘ An airplane crash or ⭘ Falling off a ship

22. Do you believe in ghosts? ⭘ No, that's silly or ⭘ Um, yes.

23. Would you stay overnight in a haunted house?

⭘ Only if my friends were with me ⭘ No way! or

⭘ Sure, I don't believe in that stuff!

24. Have you ever camped out in a cemetery?

⭘ Yes, it was cool! or ⭘ R U crazy?

25. Where do you think you'd best survive? ⭘ Sahara Desert or

⭘ Volcanic mountaintop

26. Why? _____

27. Would you rather ⭘ Scare your friends or ⭘ Be the one

getting scared?

28. What's the most dangeous thing you've ever done?

DANGER

_____

29. Were you ⭘ Nervous or ⭘ Really excited?

30. Would you do it again? ⭘ Absolutely or

⭘ No, I tried it once and that was it!

TAKING CHANCES
Living life on the edge . . .

1. ○ Skydiving or ○ Cliff diving?

2. ○ Parasailing or ○ Hang gliding?

3. ○ Rock climbing or ○ Extreme Rollerblading?

4. Would you rather ○ Be a tiger tamer or
   ○ Swim with sharks?

5. ○ Ride a bucking horse in a rodeo or
   ○ Run with the bulls?

6. ○ Go scuba diving or ○ Snorkeling?

7. ○ Walk a tightrope 50 feet in the air or
   ○ Hang by your legs from a trapeze?

8. Be a crew member ○ On a space shuttle or
   ○ On a submarine going to the bottom of the ocean?

9. ○ Drive in a NASCAR race or ○ Do some stunt-flying?

10. ○ Ski jump or ○ Surf an aerial on a big wave?

11. ○ Motorcycle or ○ Mountain bike?

12. ○ Bobsled or ○ Luge?

13. ○ Figure skating or ○ Speed skating?

14. ○ Roller coaster or ○ Ferris wheel?

15. ○ Log flume or ○ Lazy river ride?

16. ◯ Climb giant redwood trees or ◯ Hike in the Grand Canyon?

17. Fly in a ◯ Blimp or ◯ Hot air balloon?

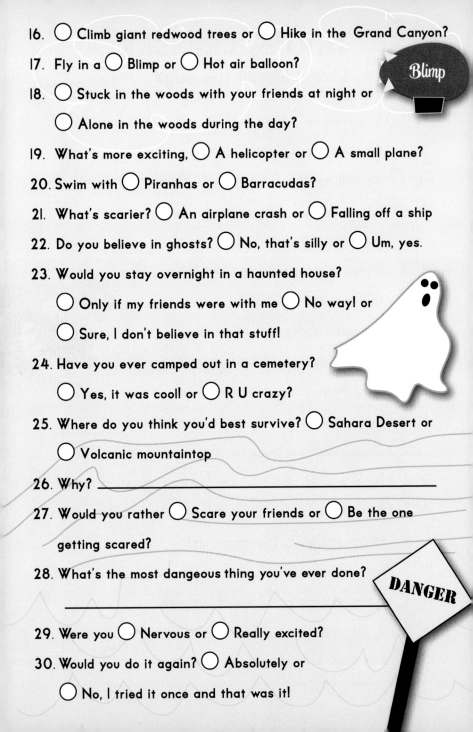

Blimp

18. ◯ Stuck in the woods with your friends at night or

◯ Alone in the woods during the day?

19. What's more exciting, ◯ A helicopter or ◯ A small plane?

20. Swim with ◯ Piranhas or ◯ Barracudas?

21. What's scarier? ◯ An airplane crash or ◯ Falling off a ship

22. Do you believe in ghosts? ◯ No, that's silly or ◯ Um, yes.

23. Would you stay overnight in a haunted house?

◯ Only if my friends were with me ◯ No way! or

◯ Sure, I don't believe in that stuff!

24. Have you ever camped out in a cemetery?

◯ Yes, it was cool! or ◯ R U crazy?

25. Where do you think you'd best survive? ◯ Sahara Desert or

◯ Volcanic mountaintop

26. Why? _____

27. Would you rather ◯ Scare your friends or ◯ Be the one

getting scared?

28. What's the most dangeous thing you've ever done?

DANGER

_____

29. Were you ◯ Nervous or ◯ Really excited?

30. Would you do it again? ◯ Absolutely or

◯ No, I tried it once and that was it!

TAKING CHANCES
Living life on the edge . . .

1. ○ Skydiving or ○ Cliff diving?

2. ○ Parasailing or ○ Hang gliding?

3. ○ Rock climbing or ○ Extreme Rollerblading?

4. Would you rather ○ Be a tiger tamer or
   ○ Swim with sharks?

5. ○ Ride a bucking horse in a rodeo or
   ○ Run with the bulls?

6. ○ Go scuba diving or ○ Snorkeling?

7. ○ Walk a tightrope 50 feet in the air or
   ○ Hang by your legs from a trapeze?

8. Be a crew member ○ On a space shuttle or
   ○ On a submarine going to the bottom of the ocean?

9. ○ Drive in a NASCAR race or ○ Do some stunt-flying?

10. ○ Ski jump or ○ Surf an aerial on a big wave?

11. ○ Motorcycle or ○ Mountain bike?

12. ○ Bobsled or ○ Luge?

13. ○ Figure skating or ○ Speed skating?

14. ○ Roller coaster or ○ Ferris wheel?

15. ○ Log flume or ○ Lazy river ride?

16. ◯ Climb giant redwood trees or ◯ Hike in the Grand Canyon?

17. Fly in a ◯ Blimp or ◯ Hot air balloon?

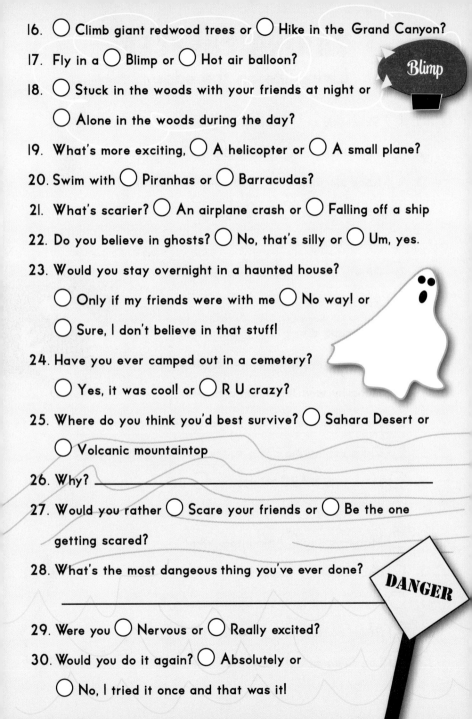

18. ◯ Stuck in the woods with your friends at night or

◯ Alone in the woods during the day?

19. What's more exciting, ◯ A helicopter or ◯ A small plane?

20. Swim with ◯ Piranhas or ◯ Barracudas?

21. What's scarier? ◯ An airplane crash or ◯ Falling off a ship

22. Do you believe in ghosts? ◯ No, that's silly or ◯ Um, yes.

23. Would you stay overnight in a haunted house?

◯ Only if my friends were with me ◯ No way! or

◯ Sure, I don't believe in that stuff!

24. Have you ever camped out in a cemetery?

◯ Yes, it was cool! or ◯ R U crazy?

25. Where do you think you'd best survive? ◯ Sahara Desert or

◯ Volcanic mountaintop

26. Why? _____

27. Would you rather ◯ Scare your friends or ◯ Be the one

getting scared?

28. What's the most dangeous thing you've ever done?

_____

29. Were you ◯ Nervous or ◯ Really excited?

30. Would you do it again? ◯ Absolutely or

◯ No, I tried it once and that was it!

TAKING CHANCES
Living life on the edge . . .

1. ◯ Skydiving or ◯ Cliff diving?

2. ◯ Parasailing or ◯ Hang gliding?

3. ◯ Rock climbing or ◯ Extreme Rollerblading?

4. Would you rather ◯ Be a tiger tamer or
   ◯ Swim with sharks?

5. ◯ Ride a bucking horse in a rodeo or
   ◯ Run with the bulls?

6. ◯ Go scuba diving or ◯ Snorkeling?

7. ◯ Walk a tightrope 50 feet in the air or
   ◯ Hang by your legs from a trapeze?

8. Be a crew member ◯ On a space shuttle or
   ◯ On a submarine going to the bottom of the ocean?

9. ◯ Drive in a NASCAR race or ◯ Do some stunt-flying?

10. ◯ Ski jump or ◯ Surf an aerial on a big wave?

11. ◯ Motorcycle or ◯ Mountain bike?

12. ◯ Bobsled or ◯ Luge?

13. ◯ Figure skating or ◯ Speed skating?

14. ◯ Roller coaster or ◯ Ferris wheel?

15. ◯ Log flume or ◯ Lazy river ride?

16. ◯ Climb giant redwood trees or ◯ Hike in the Grand Canyon?

17. Fly in a ◯ Blimp or ◯ Hot air balloon?

18. ◯ Stuck in the woods with your friends at night or

   ◯ Alone in the woods during the day?

19. What's more exciting, ◯ A helicopter or ◯ A small plane?

20. Swim with ◯ Piranhas or ◯ Barracudas?

21. What's scarier? ◯ An airplane crash or ◯ Falling off a ship

22. Do you believe in ghosts? ◯ No, that's silly or ◯ Um, yes.

23. Would you stay overnight in a haunted house?

   ◯ Only if my friends were with me ◯ No way! or

   ◯ Sure, I don't believe in that stuff!

24. Have you ever camped out in a cemetery?

   ◯ Yes, it was cool! or ◯ R U crazy?

25. Where do you think you'd best survive? ◯ Sahara Desert or

   ◯ Volcanic mountaintop

26. Why? _____

27. Would you rather ◯ Scare your friends or ◯ Be the one

   getting scared?

28. What's the most dangeous thing you've ever done?

   _____

29. Were you ◯ Nervous or ◯ Really excited?

30. Would you do it again? ◯ Absolutely or

   ◯ No, I tried it once and that was it!

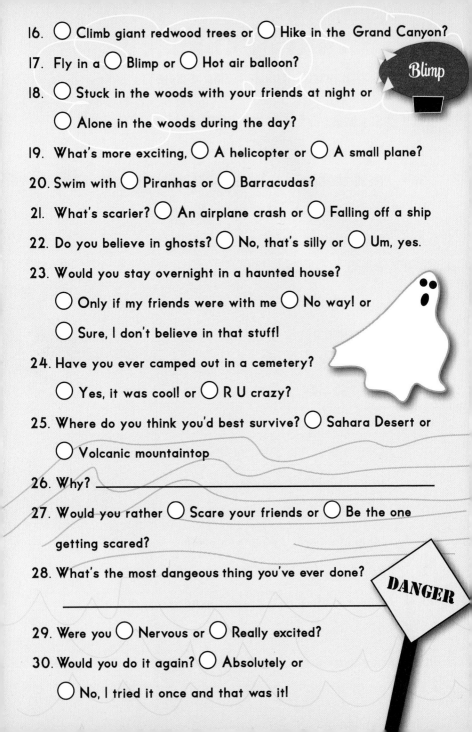

GROSS-OUT AHEAD!

Ya gotta pick one!

1. ◯ Ants in your nose or ◯ Millipedes in your ear?
2. Swim in ◯ Tomato sauce or ◯ Cough medicine?
3. ◯ Lick a New York City sidewalk or ◯ Eat your toenail clippings?
4. ◯ Be checked for lice or ◯ Check someone else?
5. Would you rather a baby ◯ Wet their diaper on you or ◯ Spit up on you?
6. ◯ Have a pet lick your mouth or ◯ Wear the same socks for a month?
7. Would you rather be buried up to your neck in ◯ Sand (sand fleas!) or ◯ Dirt (with worms!)?
8. Would you rather be in a bed full of ◯ Spiders or ◯ Cockroaches?
9. ◯ Drink camel spit or ◯ Pick up horse droppings?
10. Eat ◯ A raw egg or ◯ Raw meat?
11. ◯ Sour milk or ◯ Moldy cheese?
12. Lie down in ◯ Snail slime or ◯ Bird droppings?
13. ◯ Brush your hair with a dog's brush or ◯ Use someone else's toothbrush?
14. Eat ◯ Raw onions or ◯ Uncooked garlic?
15. ◯ Strong body odor or ◯ Scabs on your face?

16. ◯ Clean portable toilets or ◯ Inspect sewers?

17. Smell somebody's ◯ Feet or ◯ Armpits?

18. What's worse? ◯ Brown drinking water or ◯ Dead bugs on your pizza

19. ◯ A fly in your pie or ◯ A worm in your apple?

20. ◯ Washing the toilet with a toothbrush or ◯ Cleaning the kitchen floor on your hands and knees?

21. ◯ Eyeball stew or ◯ Intestinal soup?

22. What's worse? ◯ Seeing somebody pick their nose and eat it or ◯ Seeing somebody wipe their nose on their hand before giving a handshake

23. ◯ Never brush your teeth or ◯ Never shower?

24. What would be worse? ◯ Pickle-flavored ice cream or ◯ Mayonnaise gum

25. Does the sight of blood make you queasy? ◯ Yes ◯ No or ◯ I don't know

26. ◯ Blood sausage or ◯ Tripe?

27. ◯ Frostbite or ◯ Third-degree burn?

28. ◯ Foot odor or ◯ Dog breath?

29. ◯ Pop a pimple on your BFF or ◯ Brush her hair when she has bad dandruff?

30. ◯ Eat dirty snow or ◯ Drink pool water?

GROSS-OUT AHEAD!

Ya gotta pick one!

1. ⭕ Ants in your nose or ⭕ Millipedes in your ear?

2. Swim in ⭕ Tomato sauce or ⭕ Cough medicine?

3. ⭕ Lick a New York City sidewalk or ⭕ Eat your toenail clippings?

4. ⭕ Be checked for lice or ⭕ Check someone else?

5. Would you rather a baby ⭕ Wet their diaper on you or ⭕ Spit up on you?

6. ⭕ Have a pet lick your mouth or ⭕ Wear the same socks for a month?

7. Would you rather be buried up to your neck in ⭕ Sand (sand fleas!) or ⭕ Dirt (with worms!)?

8. Would you rather be in a bed full of ⭕ Spiders or ⭕ Cockroaches?

9. ⭕ Drink camel spit or ⭕ Pick up horse droppings?

10. Eat ⭕ A raw egg or ⭕ Raw meat?

11. ⭕ Sour milk or ⭕ Moldy cheese?

12. Lie down in ⭕ Snail slime or ⭕ Bird droppings?

13. ⭕ Brush your hair with a dog's brush or ⭕ Use someone else's toothbrush?

14. Eat ⭕ Raw onions or ⭕ Uncooked garlic?

15. ⭕ Strong body odor or ⭕ Scabs on your face?

16. ⚪ Clean portable toilets or ⚪ Inspect sewers?

17. Smell somebody's ⚪ Feet or ⚪ Armpits?

18. What's worse? ⚪ Brown drinking water or ⚪ Dead bugs on your pizza

19. ⚪ A fly in your pie or ⚪ A worm in your apple?

20. ⚪ Washing the toilet with a toothbrush or ⚪ Cleaning the kitchen floor on your hands and knees?

21. ⚪ Eyeball stew or ⚪ Intestinal soup?

22. What's worse? ⚪ Seeing somebody pick their nose and eat it or ⚪ Seeing somebody wipe their nose on their hand before giving a handshake

23. ⚪ Never brush your teeth or ⚪ Never shower?

24. What would be worse? ⚪ Pickle-flavored ice cream or ⚪ Mayonnaise gum

25. Does the sight of blood make you queasy? ⚪ Yes ⚪ No or ⚪ I don't know

26. ⚪ Blood sausage or ⚪ Tripe?

27. ⚪ Frostbite or ⚪ Third-degree burn?

28. ⚪ Foot odor or ⚪ Dog breath?

29. ⚪ Pop a pimple on your BFF or ⚪ Brush her hair when she has bad dandruff?

30. ⚪ Eat dirty snow or ⚪ Drink pool water?

GROSS-OUT AHEAD!
Ya gotta pick one!

1. ⭕ Ants in your nose or ⭕ Millipedes in your ear?

2. Swim in ⭕ Tomato sauce or ⭕ Cough medicine?

3. ⭕ Lick a New York City sidewalk or ⭕ Eat your toenail clippings?

4. ⭕ Be checked for lice or ⭕ Check someone else?

5. Would you rather a baby ⭕ Wet their diaper on you or ⭕ Spit up on you?

6. ⭕ Have a pet lick your mouth or ⭕ Wear the same socks for a month?

7. Would you rather be buried up to your neck in ⭕ Sand (sand fleas!) or ⭕ Dirt (with worms!)?

8. Would you rather be in a bed full of ⭕ Spiders or ⭕ Cockroaches?

9. ⭕ Drink camel spit or ⭕ Pick up horse droppings?

10. Eat ⭕ A raw egg or ⭕ Raw meat?

11. ⭕ Sour milk or ⭕ Moldy cheese?

12. Lie down in ⭕ Snail slime or ⭕ Bird droppings?

13. ⭕ Brush your hair with a dog's brush or ⭕ Use someone else's toothbrush?

14. Eat ⭕ Raw onions or ⭕ Uncooked garlic?

15. ⭕ Strong body odor or ⭕ Scabs on your face?

16. ⚪ Clean portable toilets or ⚪ Inspect sewers?

17. Smell somebody's ⚪ Feet or ⚪ Armpits?

18. What's worse? ⚪ Brown drinking water or ⚪ Dead bugs on your pizza

19. ⚪ A fly in your pie or ⚪ A worm in your apple?

20. ⚪ Washing the toilet with a toothbrush or ⚪ Cleaning the kitchen floor on your hands and knees?

21. ⚪ Eyeball stew or ⚪ Intestinal soup?

22. What's worse? ⚪ Seeing somebody pick their nose and eat it or ⚪ Seeing somebody wipe their nose on their hand before giving a handshake

23. ⚪ Never brush your teeth or ⚪ Never shower?

24. What would be worse? ⚪ Pickle-flavored ice cream or ⚪ Mayonnaise gum

25. Does the sight of blood make you queasy? ⚪ Yes ⚪ No or ⚪ I don't know

26. ⚪ Blood sausage or ⚪ Tripe?

27. ⚪ Frostbite or ⚪ Third-degree burn?

28. ⚪ Foot odor or ⚪ Dog breath?

29. ⚪ Pop a pimple on your BFF or ⚪ Brush her hair when she has bad dandruff?

30. ⚪ Eat dirty snow or ⚪ Drink pool water?

GROSS-OUT AHEAD!

Ya gotta pick one!

1. ◯ Ants in your nose or ◯ Millipedes in your ear?

2. Swim in ◯ Tomato sauce or ◯ Cough medicine?

3. ◯ Lick a New York City sidewalk or ◯ Eat your toenail clippings?

4. ◯ Be checked for lice or ◯ Check someone else?

5. Would you rather a baby ◯ Wet their diaper on you or ◯ Spit up on you?

6. ◯ Have a pet lick your mouth or ◯ Wear the same socks for a month?

7. Would you rather be buried up to your neck in ◯ Sand (sand fleas!) or ◯ Dirt (with worms!)?

8. Would you rather be in a bed full of ◯ Spiders or ◯ Cockroaches?

9. ◯ Drink camel spit or ◯ Pick up horse droppings?

10. Eat ◯ A raw egg or ◯ Raw meat?

11. ◯ Sour milk or ◯ Moldy cheese?

12. Lie down in ◯ Snail slime or ◯ Bird droppings?

13. ◯ Brush your hair with a dog's brush or ◯ Use someone else's toothbrush?

14. Eat ◯ Raw onions or ◯ Uncooked garlic?

15. ◯ Strong body odor or ◯ Scabs on your face?

16. ⭕ Clean portable toilets or ⭕ Inspect sewers?

17. Smell somebody's ⭕ Feet or ⭕ Armpits?

18. What's worse? ⭕ Brown drinking water or ⭕ Dead bugs on your pizza

19. ⭕ A fly in your pie or ⭕ A worm in your apple?

20. ⭕ Washing the toilet with a toothbrush or ⭕ Cleaning the kitchen floor on your hands and knees?

21. ⭕ Eyeball stew or ⭕ Intestinal soup?

22. What's worse? ⭕ Seeing somebody pick their nose and eat it or ⭕ Seeing somebody wipe their nose on their hand before giving a handshake

23. ⭕ Never brush your teeth or ⭕ Never shower?

24. What would be worse? ⭕ Pickle-flavored ice cream or ⭕ Mayonnaise gum

25. Does the sight of blood make you queasy? ⭕ Yes ⭕ No or ⭕ I don't know

26. ⭕ Blood sausage or ⭕ Tripe?

27. ⭕ Frostbite or ⭕ Third-degree burn?

28. ⭕ Foot odor or ⭕ Dog breath?

29. ⭕ Pop a pimple on your BFF or ⭕ Brush her hair when she has bad dandruff?

30. ⭕ Eat dirty snow or ⭕ Drink pool water?

CREATIVITY CORNER
What you like to do to express yourself

1. What do you think are your hidden artistic talents?

   _____

2. ○ Does anyone else know or ○ Do you keep them a secret?

3. ○ Sing out loud or ○ Only in the shower?

4. If you can sing, have you sung in front of people other than your family? ○ Yes or ○ No, it's my little secret.

5. ○ Sing a solo or ○ Stay in the chorus?

6. Write ○ A song or ○ A novel?

7. Who is your favorite author?_____

8. Write ○ Poetry or ○ A magazine article?

9. Do you like poetry? ○ Yes or ○ Ugh!

10. Who is your favorite poet?_____

11. What is your fave magazine? _____

12. ○ Design a new clothing line or ○ Walk the catwalk?

13. Fave model? _____

14. Fave designer? _____

15. ○ Debater or ○ Moderator?

16. In soccer: ⃝ Most assists or ⃝ Most goals?

17. ⃝ Break-dance or ⃝ Waltz?

18. ⃝ Ballet or ⃝ Salsa?

19. ⃝ Painting or ⃝ Photography?

20. What kind of pictures do you prefer to take?

    ⃝ Portraits or ⃝ Scenic

21. ⃝ Sew or ⃝ Knit?

22. ⃝ Act in the school play or ⃝ Be on the stage crew?

23. ⃝ Play an instrument or ⃝ Review music?

24. ⃝ Write books or ⃝ Review books?

25. ⃝ Doctor or ⃝ Veterinarian?

26. ⃝ Architect or ⃝ Interior decorator?

27. ⃝ Defense attorney or ⃝ Prosecutor?

28. ⃝ Design your own video game or ⃝ Develop a whole new game system?

29. Be a ⃝ Chef or ⃝ Maitre d'?

30. ⃝ Invent the hottest new gadget or ⃝ Advertise the hottest new gadget?

CREATIVITY CORNER
What you like to do to express yourself

1. What do you think are your hidden artistic talents?

   _____

2. ○ Does anyone else know or ○ Do you keep them a secret?

3. ○ Sing out loud or ○ Only in the shower?

4. If you can sing, have you sung in front of people other than your family? ○ Yes or ○ No, it's my little secret.

5. ○ Sing a solo or ○ Stay in the chorus?

6. Write ○ A song or ○ A novel?

7. Who is your favorite author?_____

8. Write ○ Poetry or ○ A magazine article?

9. Do you like poetry? ○ Yes or ○ Ugh!

10. Who is your favorite poet?_____

11. What is your fave magazine? _____

12. ○ Design a new clothing line or ○ Walk the catwalk?

13. Fave model? _____

14. Fave designer? _____

15. ○ Debater or ○ Moderator?

16. In soccer: ◯ Most assists or ◯ Most goals?

17. ◯ Break-dance or ◯ Waltz?

18. ◯ Ballet or ◯ Salsa?

19. ◯ Painting or ◯ Photography?

20. What kind of pictures do you prefer to take?

    ◯ Portraits or ◯ Scenic

21. ◯ Sew or ◯ Knit?

22. ◯ Act in the school play or ◯ Be on the stage crew?

23. ◯ Play an instrument or ◯ Review music?

24. ◯ Write books or ◯ Review books?

25. ◯ Doctor or ◯ Veterinarian?

26. ◯ Architect or ◯ Interior decorator?

27. ◯ Defense attorney or ◯ Prosecutor?

28. ◯ Design your own video game or ◯ Develop a whole new game system?

29. Be a ◯ Chef or ◯ Maitre d'?

30. ◯ Invent the hottest new gadget or ◯ Advertise the hottest new gadget?

CREATIVITY CORNER
What you like to do to express yourself

1. What do you think are your hidden artistic talents?

   _____

2. ○ Does anyone else know or ○ Do you keep them a secret?

3. ○ Sing out loud or ○ Only in the shower?

4. If you can sing, have you sung in front of people other than your family? ○ Yes or ○ No, it's my little secret.

5. ○ Sing a solo or ○ Stay in the chorus?

6. Write ○ A song or ○ A novel?

7. Who is your favorite author?_____

8. Write ○ Poetry or ○ A magazine article?

9. Do you like poetry? ○ Yes or ○ Ugh!

10. Who is your favorite poet?_____

11. What is your fave magazine? _____

12. ○ Design a new clothing line or ○ Walk the catwalk?

13. Fave model? _____

14. Fave designer? _____

15. ○ Debater or ○ Moderator?

16. In soccer: ◯ Most assists or ◯ Most goals?

17. ◯ Break-dance or ◯ Waltz?

18. ◯ Ballet or ◯ Salsa?

19. ◯ Painting or ◯ Photography?

20. What kind of pictures do you prefer to take?

    ◯ Portraits or ◯ Scenic

21. ◯ Sew or ◯ Knit?

22. ◯ Act in the school play or ◯ Be on the stage crew?

23. ◯ Play an instrument or ◯ Review music?

24. ◯ Write books or ◯ Review books?

25. ◯ Doctor or ◯ Veterinarian?

26. ◯ Architect or ◯ Interior decorator?

27. ◯ Defense attorney or ◯ Prosecutor?

28. ◯ Design your own video game or ◯ Develop a whole new game system?

29. Be a ◯ Chef or ◯ Maitre d'?

30. ◯ Invent the hottest new gadget or ◯ Advertise the hottest new gadget?

CREATIVITY CORNER
What you like to do to express yourself

1. What do you think are your hidden artistic talents?

   _____

2. ○ Does anyone else know or ○ Do you keep them a secret?

3. ○ Sing out loud or ○ Only in the shower?

4. If you can sing, have you sung in front of people other than your family? ○ Yes or ○ No, it's my little secret.

5. ○ Sing a solo or ○ Stay in the chorus?

6. Write ○ A song or ○ A novel?

7. Who is your favorite author?_____

8. Write ○ Poetry or ○ A magazine article?

9. Do you like poetry? ○ Yes or ○ Ugh!

10. Who is your favorite poet?_____

11. What is your fave magazine? _____

12. ○ Design a new clothing line or ○ Walk the catwalk?

13. Fave model? _____

14. Fave designer? _____

15. ○ Debater or ○ Moderator?

16. In soccer: ◯ Most assists or ◯ Most goals?

17. ◯ Break-dance or ◯ Waltz?

18. ◯ Ballet or ◯ Salsa?

19. ◯ Painting or ◯ Photography?

20. What kind of pictures do you prefer to take?

    ◯ Portraits or ◯ Scenic

21. ◯ Sew or ◯ Knit?

22. ◯ Act in the school play or ◯ Be on the stage crew?

23. ◯ Play an instrument or ◯ Review music?

24. ◯ Write books or ◯ Review books?

25. ◯ Doctor or ◯ Veterinarian?

26. ◯ Architect or ◯ Interior decorator?

27. ◯ Defense attorney or ◯ Prosecutor?

28. ◯ Design your own video game or ◯ Develop a whole new game system?

29. Be a ◯ Chef or ◯ Maitre d'?

30. ◯ Invent the hottest new gadget or ◯ Advertise the hottest new gadget?

most embarrassing moments

Things work out in the end . . .

1. What happens to you when you get embarrassed?

   ◯ Blush beet red ◯ Turn pale as a sheet ◯ Get sweaty palms

   ◯ Can't speak or ◯ Laugh uncontrollably

2. What's your most embarrassing moment?

   _____

3. What's worse? ◯ Your crush finds out you like him or

   ◯ Your friends talk about you behind your back

4. ◯ Fail a class for the semester or ◯ Lose your BFF?

5. ◯ Say the wrong answer in class or ◯ Trip onstage

   during a play?

6. ◯ Have a bad yearbook picture or ◯ Nobody signs it?

7. ◯ Huge stain on your shirt or ◯ Something green in your teeth?

8. ◯ Being a kiss-up or ◯ Detention for talking?

9. ◯ Your sneaker flies off and hits your coach or

   ◯ You fall off your chair in the middle of class?

10. ◯ Waltz with your crush or ◯ Write him a poem?

11. ◯ Fall asleep in class or ◯ Lose a spelling bee?

12. ◯ Forget your lines in a play or ◯ Burp in public?

13. ◯ Call a teacher "Mom" or ◯ Snort-laugh?

14. Get caught ◯ Staring at your crush or ◯ Daydreaming?

15. Sitting ◯ In a puddle of water or ◯ On melted chocolate?

16. ⃝ Sneeze on a teacher or ⃝ Hiccup during silent reading?

17. What is worse in front of your crush? ⃝ Something hanging out of your nose or ⃝ Falling down

18. Fall face-first ⃝ Into snow or ⃝ On a beach?

19. If your bathing suit gets pulled down, what do you do?
⃝ Scream for a towel or ⃝ Laugh and pull it back up

20. ⃝ A pimple on your nose or ⃝ A stain on your pants?

21. ⃝ Toilet paper on your shoe or ⃝ Forget to zip your pants?

22. ⃝ Wearing clothes from the hamper or ⃝ Getting hit in the head?

23. Getting yelled at by ⃝ Your parents in front of your friends or ⃝ Your teacher in class?

24. ⃝ Your mother calls you an embarrassing nickname or ⃝ Your little sister tells a boy you like him?

25. What's worse? ⃝ Mom reading your diary or ⃝ Your crush reading it

26. What's worse? ⃝ Ripped pants or ⃝ A ripped shirt

27. ⃝ Your blog gets posted on the school website or ⃝ Your crush says he doesn't like you?

28. ⃝ Spit while talking to your crush or ⃝ Sneeze on him?

29. ⃝ Your shirt goes up in gym class or ⃝ Your shorts fall down as you're climbing the rope?

30. Ever snorted a drink out your nose? ⃝ Sure or ⃝ Never!

most Embarrassing moments

Things work out in the end...

1. What happens to you when you get embarrassed?

   ○ Blush beet red ○ Turn pale as a sheet ○ Get sweaty palms

   ○ Can't speak or ○ Laugh uncontrollably

2. What's your most embarrassing moment?

   _____

3. What's worse? ○ Your crush finds out you like him or

   ○ Your friends talk about you behind your back

4. ○ Fail a class for the semester or ○ Lose your BFF?

5. ○ Say the wrong answer in class or ○ Trip onstage

   during a play?

6. ○ Have a bad yearbook picture or ○ Nobody signs it?

7. ○ Huge stain on your shirt or ○ Something green in your teeth?

8. ○ Being a kiss-up or ○ Detention for talking?

9. ○ Your sneaker flies off and hits your coach or

   ○ You fall off your chair in the middle of class?

10. ○ Waltz with your crush or ○ Write him a poem?

11. ○ Fall asleep in class or ○ Lose a spelling bee?

12. ○ Forget your lines in a play or ○ Burp in public?

13. ○ Call a teacher "Mom" or ○ Snort-laugh?

14. Get caught ○ Staring at your crush or ○ Daydreaming?

15. Sitting ○ In a puddle of water or ○ On melted chocolate?

16. ○ Sneeze on a teacher or ○ Hiccup during silent reading?

17. What is worse in front of your crush? ○ Something hanging out of your nose or ○ Falling down

18. Fall face-first ○ Into snow or ○ On a beach?

19. If your bathing suit gets pulled down, what do you do?
○ Scream for a towel or ○ Laugh and pull it back up

20. ○ A pimple on your nose or ○ A stain on your pants?

21. ○ Toilet paper on your shoe or ○ Forget to zip your pants?

22. ○ Wearing clothes from the hamper or ○ Getting hit in the head?

23. Getting yelled at by ○ Your parents in front of your friends or ○ Your teacher in class?

24. ○ Your mother calls you an embarrassing nickname or ○ Your little sister tells a boy you like him?

25. What's worse? ○ Mom reading your diary or ○ Your crush reading it

26. What's worse? ○ Ripped pants or ○ A ripped shirt

27. ○ Your blog gets posted on the school website or ○ Your crush says he doesn't like you?

28. ○ Spit while talking to your crush or ○ Sneeze on him?

29. ○ Your shirt goes up in gym class or ○ Your shorts fall down as you're climbing the rope?

30. Ever snorted a drink out your nose? ○ Sure or ○ Never!

most EmbarRassing momEnts

Things work out in the end . . .

1. What happens to you when you get embarrassed?

   ◯ Blush beet red ◯ Turn pale as a sheet ◯ Get sweaty palms

   ◯ Can't speak or ◯ Laugh uncontrollably

2. What's your most embarrassing moment?

   _____

3. What's worse? ◯ Your crush finds out you like him or

   ◯ Your friends talk about you behind your back

4. ◯ Fail a class for the semester or ◯ Lose your BFF?

5. ◯ Say the wrong answer in class or ◯ Trip onstage

   during a play?

6. ◯ Have a bad yearbook picture or ◯ Nobody signs it?

7. ◯ Huge stain on your shirt or ◯ Something green in your teeth?

8. ◯ Being a kiss-up or ◯ Detention for talking?

9. ◯ Your sneaker flies off and hits your coach or

   ◯ You fall off your chair in the middle of class?

10. ◯ Waltz with your crush or ◯ Write him a poem?

11. ◯ Fall asleep in class or ◯ Lose a spelling bee?

12. ◯ Forget your lines in a play or ◯ Burp in public?

13. ◯ Call a teacher "Mom" or ◯ Snort-laugh?

14. Get caught ◯ Staring at your crush or ◯ Daydreaming?

15. Sitting ◯ In a puddle of water or ◯ On melted chocolate?

16. ⚪ Sneeze on a teacher or ⚪ Hiccup during silent reading?

17. What is worse in front of your crush? ⚪ Something hanging out of your nose or ⚪ Falling down

18. Fall face-first ⚪ Into snow or ⚪ On a beach?

19. If your bathing suit gets pulled down, what do you do?
    ⚪ Scream for a towel or ⚪ Laugh and pull it back up

20. ⚪ A pimple on your nose or ⚪ A stain on your pants?

21. ⚪ Toilet paper on your shoe or ⚪ Forget to zip your pants?

22. ⚪ Wearing clothes from the hamper or ⚪ Getting hit in the head?

23. Getting yelled at by ⚪ Your parents in front of your friends or ⚪ Your teacher in class?

24. ⚪ Your mother calls you an embarrassing nickname or ⚪ Your little sister tells a boy you like him?

25. What's worse? ⚪ Mom reading your diary or ⚪ Your crush reading it

26. What's worse? ⚪ Ripped pants or ⚪ A ripped shirt

27. ⚪ Your blog gets posted on the school website or ⚪ Your crush says he doesn't like you?

28. ⚪ Spit while talking to your crush or ⚪ Sneeze on him?

29. ⚪ Your shirt goes up in gym class or ⚪ Your shorts fall down as you're climbing the rope?

30. Ever snorted a drink out your nose? ⚪ Sure or ⚪ Never!

most Embarrassing moments

Things work out in the end . . .

1. What happens to you when you get embarrassed?

   ◯ Blush beet red ◯ Turn pale as a sheet ◯ Get sweaty palms

   ◯ Can't speak or ◯ Laugh uncontrollably

2. What's your most embarrassing moment?

   _____

3. What's worse? ◯ Your crush finds out you like him or

   ◯ Your friends talk about you behind your back

4. ◯ Fail a class for the semester or ◯ Lose your BFF?

5. ◯ Say the wrong answer in class or ◯ Trip onstage

   during a play?

6. ◯ Have a bad yearbook picture or ◯ Nobody signs it?

7. ◯ Huge stain on your shirt or ◯ Something green in your teeth?

8. ◯ Being a kiss-up or ◯ Detention for talking?

9. ◯ Your sneaker flies off and hits your coach or

   ◯ You fall off your chair in the middle of class?

10. ◯ Waltz with your crush or ◯ Write him a poem?

11. ◯ Fall asleep in class or ◯ Lose a spelling bee?

12. ◯ Forget your lines in a play or ◯ Burp in public?

13. ◯ Call a teacher "Mom" or ◯ Snort-laugh?

14. Get caught ◯ Staring at your crush or ◯ Daydreaming?

15. Sitting ◯ In a puddle of water or ◯ On melted chocolate?

16. ⭕ Sneeze on a teacher or ⭕ Hiccup during silent reading?

17. What is worse in front of your crush? ⭕ Something hanging out of your nose or ⭕ Falling down

18. Fall face-first ⭕ Into snow or ⭕ On a beach?

19. If your bathing suit gets pulled down, what do you do? ⭕ Scream for a towel or ⭕ Laugh and pull it back up

20. ⭕ A pimple on your nose or ⭕ A stain on your pants?

21. ⭕ Toilet paper on your shoe or ⭕ Forget to zip your pants?

22. ⭕ Wearing clothes from the hamper or ⭕ Getting hit in the head?

23. Getting yelled at by ⭕ Your parents in front of your friends or ⭕ Your teacher in class?

24. ⭕ Your mother calls you an embarrassing nickname or ⭕ Your little sister tells a boy you like him?

25. What's worse? ⭕ Mom reading your diary or ⭕ Your crush reading it

26. What's worse? ⭕ Ripped pants or ⭕ A ripped shirt

27. ⭕ Your blog gets posted on the school website or ⭕ Your crush says he doesn't like you?

28. ⭕ Spit while talking to your crush or ⭕ Sneeze on him?

29. ⭕ Your shirt goes up in gym class or ⭕ Your shorts fall down as you're climbing the rope?

30. Ever snorted a drink out your nose? ⭕ Sure or ⭕ Never!

Random Thoughts

More questions to share with your friends!

1. ◯ Photographs or ◯ Videos?

2. ◯ Candy canes or ◯ Lollipops?

3. ◯ White roses or ◯ Red?

4. ◯ Action video games or ◯ Puzzle video games?

5. ◯ Water or ◯ Energy drink?

6. ◯ Facebook or ◯ MySpace?

7. What's your fave way to communicate?_____

8. If you won a million dollars, what would be the first

    thing you'd do? _____

9. Would you share your million with family and friends?

    ◯ Yes! It's not like I worked for it or ◯ No way, it's mine!

    or ◯ Maybe if they needed it.

10. Do you keep up with current events? ◯ Yes or ◯ No

11. What's your favorite way to eat peanut butter?

    _____

12. Nail polish: ◯ Red ◯ Pink ◯ Other or ◯ None?

13. ◯ Laptop or ◯ Desktop?

14. ◯ PC or ◯ Mac?

15. ◯ Escalator or ◯ Elevator?

16. Would you rather live in ◯ Alaska or ◯ Hawaii?

17. Would you rather ◯ Walk or ◯ Ride your bike?

18. Would you rather get ◯ Your hair cut and styled or
    ◯ A manicure/pedicure?

19. Skiing: ◯ Water or ◯ Snow?

20. Jewelry: ◯ Gold or ◯ Silver?

21. ◯ Dangling earrings or ◯ Studs?

22. Would you rather ◯ Play a sport or ◯ Be a spectator?

23. ◯ Play on a losing team or ◯ Sit on the bench of a
    winning team?

24. If you had to choose, would you rather be ◯ Blind or
    ◯ Deaf?

25. ◯ Six toes on each foot or ◯ Six fingers on each hand?

26. ◯ Marry your true love or ◯ Win the lottery?

27. Survive in the desert ◯ Alone or ◯ With your worst enemy?

28. Would you rather ◯ You had amnesia or ◯ Everyone
    forgot about you?

29. ◯ Three eyes or ◯ Two noses?

30. ◯ Everyone making fun of you or ◯ Nobody noticing
    you at all?

Random Thoughts

More questions to share with your friends!

1. ◯ Photographs or ◯ Videos?

2. ◯ Candy canes or ◯ Lollipops?

3. ◯ White roses or ◯ Red?

4. ◯ Action video games or ◯ Puzzle video games?

5. ◯ Water or ◯ Energy drink?

6. ◯ Facebook or ◯ MySpace?

7. What's your fave way to communicate?_____

8. If you won a million dollars, what would be the first

    thing you'd do? _____

9. Would you share your million with family and friends?

    ◯ Yes! It's not like I worked for it or ◯ No way, it's mine!

    or ◯ Maybe if they needed it.

10. Do you keep up with current events? ◯ Yes or ◯ No.

11. What's your favorite way to eat peanut butter?

    _____

12. Nail polish: ◯ Red ◯ Pink ◯ Other or ◯ None?

13. ◯ Laptop or ◯ Desktop?

14. ◯ PC or ◯ Mac?

15. ◯ Escalator or ◯ Elevator?

16. Would you rather live in ⭘ Alaska or ⭘ Hawaii?

17. Would you rather ⭘ Walk or ⭘ Ride your bike?

18. Would you rather get ⭘ Your hair cut and styled or
⭘ A manicure/pedicure?

19. Skiing: ⭘ Water or ⭘ Snow?

20. Jewelry: ⭘ Gold or ⭘ Silver?

21. ⭘ Dangling earrings or ⭘ Studs?

22. Would you rather ⭘ Play a sport or ⭘ Be a spectator?

23. ⭘ Play on a losing team or ⭘ Sit on the bench of a
winning team?

24. If you had to choose, would you rather be ⭘ Blind or
⭘ Deaf?

25. ⭘ Six toes on each foot or ⭘ Six fingers on each hand?

26. ⭘ Marry your true love or ⭘ Win the lottery?

27. Survive in the desert ⭘ Alone or ⭘ With your worst enemy?

28. Would you rather ⭘ You had amnesia or ⭘ Everyone
forgot about you?

29. ⭘ Three eyes or ⭘ Two noses?

30. ⭘ Everyone making fun of you or ⭘ Nobody noticing
you at all?

Random Thoughts

More questions to share with your friends!

1. ⭘ Photographs or ⭘ Videos?

2. ⭘ Candy canes or ⭘ Lollipops?

3. ⭘ White roses or ⭘ Red?

4. ⭘ Action video games or ⭘ Puzzle video games?

5. ⭘ Water or ⭘ Energy drink?

6. ⭘ Facebook or ⭘ MySpace?

7. What's your fave way to communicate?_____

8. If you won a million dollars, what would be the first

   thing you'd do? _____

9. Would you share your million with family and friends?

   ⭘ Yes! It's not like I worked for it or ⭘ No way, it's mine!

   or ⭘ Maybe if they needed it.

10. Do you keep up with current events? ⭘ Yes or ⭘ No.

11. What's your favorite way to eat peanut butter?

    _____

12. Nail polish: ⭘ Red ⭘ Pink ⭘ Other or ⭘ None?

13. ⭘ Laptop or ⭘ Desktop?

14. ⭘ PC or ⭘ Mac?

15. ⭘ Escalator or ⭘ Elevator?

16. Would you rather live in ◯ Alaska or ◯ Hawaii?

17. Would you rather ◯ Walk or ◯ Ride your bike?

18. Would you rather get ◯ Your hair cut and styled or

    ◯ A manicure/pedicure?

19. Skiing: ◯ Water or ◯ Snow?

20. Jewelry: ◯ Gold or ◯ Silver?

21. ◯ Dangling earrings or ◯ Studs?

22. Would you rather ◯ Play a sport or ◯ Be a spectator?

23. ◯ Play on a losing team or ◯ Sit on the bench of a

    winning team?

24. If you had to choose, would you rather be ◯ Blind or

    ◯ Deaf?

25. ◯ Six toes on each foot or ◯ Six fingers on each hand?

26. ◯ Marry your true love or ◯ Win the lottery?

27. Survive in the desert ◯ Alone or ◯ With your worst enemy?

28. Would you rather ◯ You had amnesia or ◯ Everyone

    forgot about you?

29. ◯ Three eyes or ◯ Two noses?

30. ◯ Everyone making fun of you or ◯ Nobody noticing

    you at all?

Random Thoughts

More questions to share with your friends!

1. ◯ Photographs or ◯ Videos?

2. ◯ Candy canes or ◯ Lollipops?

3. ◯ White roses or ◯ Red?

4. ◯ Action video games or ◯ Puzzle video games?

5. ◯ Water or ◯ Energy drink?

6. ◯ Facebook or ◯ MySpace?

7. What's your fave way to communicate?_____

8. If you won a million dollars, what would be the first

   thing you'd do? _____

9. Would you share your million with family and friends?

   ◯ Yes! It's not like I worked for it or ◯ No way, it's mine!

   or ◯ Maybe if they needed it.

10. Do you keep up with current events? ◯ Yes or ◯ No

11. What's your favorite way to eat peanut butter?

    _____

12. Nail polish: ◯ Red ◯ Pink ◯ Other or ◯ None?

13. ◯ Laptop or ◯ Desktop?

14. ◯ PC or ◯ Mac?

15. ◯ Escalator or ◯ Elevator?

16. Would you rather live in ◯ Alaska or ◯ Hawaii?

17. Would you rather ◯ Walk or ◯ Ride your bike?

18. Would you rather get ◯ Your hair cut and styled or
    ◯ A manicure/pedicure?

19. Skiing: ◯ Water or ◯ Snow?

20. Jewelry: ◯ Gold or ◯ Silver?

21. ◯ Dangling earrings or ◯ Studs?

22. Would you rather ◯ Play a sport or ◯ Be a spectator?

23. ◯ Play on a losing team or ◯ Sit on the bench of a
    winning team?

24. If you had to choose, would you rather be ◯ Blind or
    ◯ Deaf?

25. ◯ Six toes on each foot or ◯ Six fingers on each hand?

26. ◯ Marry your true love or ◯ Win the lottery?

27. Survive in the desert ◯ Alone or ◯ With your worst enemy?

28. Would you rather ◯ You had amnesia or ◯ Everyone
    forgot about you?

29. ◯ Three eyes or ◯ Two noses?

30. ◯ Everyone making fun of you or ◯ Nobody noticing
    you at all?

FOR BFFS' EYES ONLY

WHAT DO YOU GUYS KNOW ABOUT EACH OTHER?

1. What is your earliest memory?_____

_____

2. What was your first word?_____

3. What gives you nightmares?_____

4. Afraid of the dark? ◯ Sometimes ◯ Yup or ◯ Nope

5. Would you still color with crayons? ◯ No way,

   crayons are for babies or ◯ Yes, I love the colors!

6. Do you watch the latest animated movies? ◯ Yes

   or ◯ Only with little kids!

7. Did you have a fave stuffed animal? ◯ Yes or ◯ No

8. Do you still have it? ◯ No ◯ Yes! ◯ Shh, don't tell!

9. What was your BFF's fave stuffed animal?

_____

10. Does she still have it? ◯ Yes or ◯ No way!

11. Do you still play board games togther? ◯ No! or ◯ Sure!

12. Do you have a crush? ◯ Yes or ◯ I'm not telling!

13. Does he know? ◯ No or ◯ Not unless my BFF tells him

14. Have you ever gone to a sports game just to see your

    crush? ◯ Yes ◯ No, I only go for the game!

15. Do you wish you could live with your best friend's

    family? ◯ Yes ◯ No or ◯ Sometimes

16. Has your BFF taken the blame for you? ◯ Yes or ◯ No

17. Have you for her? ◯ Yes or ◯ No

18. Are you ◯ Clumsy or ◯ Graceful?

19. Do you laugh at the same things? ◯ Always or ◯ Sometimes

20. ◯ Peacemaker or ◯ Always wait for your BFF to apologize?

21. If your pants ripped in school, would you ◯ Insist on going home or ◯ Wrap a sweater around your waist and stay?

22. What would your BFF do?_____

23. If you saw someone famous, would you ◯ Run up to them for an autograph or ◯ Hang back, giggling?

24. Would your BFF ◯ Approach a famous person or ◯ Not?

25. If your BFF fell down the stairs, would you ◯ Blush or ◯ Laugh?

26. Would your BFF ◯ Blush or ◯ Laugh?

27. Tell your BFF she has body odor? ◯ Yes or ◯ No, that's too embarrassing.

28. Would you want your BFF to tell you if you had bad body odor? ◯ Absolutely or ◯ No!

29. You just ate sour cream and onion chips and as you talk to your crush you realize your breath smells. What do you do? ◯ Admit it and ask for gum or ◯ Cover your mouth and run

30. And your BFF? Would she ◯ Admit it or ◯ Run?

FOR BFFS' EYES ONLY

WHAT DO YOU GUYS KNOW ABOUT EACH OTHER?

1. What is your earliest memory?_____

   _____

2. What was your first word?_____

3. What gives you nightmares?_____

4. Afraid of the dark? ◯ Sometimes ◯ Yup or ◯ Nope

5. Would you still color with crayons? ◯ No way, crayons are for babies or ◯ Yes, I love the colors!

6. Do you watch the latest animated movies? ◯ Yes or ◯ Only with little kids!

7. Did you have a fave stuffed animal? ◯ Yes or ◯ No

8. Do you still have it? ◯ No ◯ Yes! ◯ Shh, don't tell!

9. What was your BFF's fave stuffed animal?

   _____

10. Does she still have it? ◯ Yes or ◯ No way!

11. Do you still play board games togther? ◯ No! or ◯ Sure!

12. Do you have a crush? ◯ Yes or ◯ I'm not telling!

13. Does he know? ◯ No or ◯ Not unless my BFF tells him

14. Have you ever gone to a sports game just to see your crush? ◯ Yes ◯ No, I only go for the game!

15. Do you wish you could live with your best friend's family? ◯ Yes ◯ No or ◯ Sometimes

16. Has your BFF taken the blame for you? ◯ Yes or ◯ No

17. Have you for her? ◯ Yes or ◯ No

18. Are you ◯ Clumsy or ◯ Graceful?

19. Do you laugh at the same things? ◯ Always or ◯ Sometimes

20. ◯ Peacemaker or ◯ Always wait for your BFF to apologize?

21. If your pants ripped in school, would you ◯ Insist on going home or ◯ Wrap a sweater around your waist and stay?

22. What would your BFF do?_____

23. If you saw someone famous, would you ◯ Run up to them for an autograph or ◯ Hang back, giggling?

24. Would your BFF ◯ Approach a famous person or ◯ Not?

25. If your BFF fell down the stairs, would you ◯ Blush or ◯ Laugh?

26. Would your BFF ◯ Blush or ◯ Laugh?

27. Tell your BFF she has body odor? ◯ Yes or ◯ No, that's too embarrassing.

28. Would you want your BFF to tell you if you had bad body odor? ◯ Absolutely or ◯ No!

29. You just ate sour cream and onion chips and as you talk to your crush you realize your breath smells. What do you do? ◯ Admit it and ask for gum or ◯ Cover your mouth and run

30. And your BFF? Would she ◯ Admit it or ◯ Run?